AF435522

A Child's History of

Abraham Lincoln

James Gardner

CONTENTS

ABRAHAM LINCOLN.

THE STORY OF ABRAHAM LINCOLN.

I.—The Kentucky Home.

Not far from Hodgensville, in Kentucky, there once lived a man whose name was Thomas Lincoln. This man had built for himself a little log cabin by the side of a brook, where there was an ever-flowing spring of water.

There was but one room in this cabin. On the side next to the brook there was a low doorway; and at one end there was a large fireplace, built of rough stones and clay.

The chimney was very broad at the bottom and narrow at the top. It was made of clay, with flat stones and slender sticks laid around the outside to keep it from falling apart.

In the wall, on one side of the fireplace, there was a square hole for a window. But there was no glass in this window. In the summer it was left open all the time. In cold weather a deer-skin, or a piece of coarse cloth, was hung over it to keep out the wind and the snow.

At night, or on stormy days, the skin of a bear was hung across the doorway ; for there was no door on hinges to be opened and shut.

There was no ceiling to the room. But the inmates of the cabin, by looking up, could see the bare rafters and the rough roof-boards, which Mr. Lincoln himself had split and hewn.

There was no floor, but only the bare ground that had been smoothed and beaten until it was as level and hard as pavement.

For chairs there were only blocks of wood and a rude bench on one side of the fireplace. The bed was a little platform of poles, on which were spread the furry skins of wild animals, and a patchwork quilt of homespun goods.

In this poor cabin, on the 12th of February, 1809, a baby boy was born. There was already one child in the family—a girl, two years old, whose name was Sarah.

The little boy grew and became strong like

other babies, and his parents named him Abra-. ham, after his grandfather, who had been killed by the Indians many years before.

When he was old enough to run about, he liked to play under the trees by the cabin door. Sometimes he would go with his little sister into the woods and watch the birds and the squirrels.

He had no playmates. He did not know the meaning of toys or playthings. But he was a happy child and had many pleasant ways.

Thomas Lincoln, the father, was a kind-hearted man, very strong and brave. Sometimes he would take the child on his knee and tell him strange, true stories of the great forest, and of the Indians and the fierce beasts that roamed among the woods and hills.

For Thomas Lincoln had always lived on the wild frontier; and he would rather hunt deer and other game in the forest than do anything else. Perhaps this is why he was so poor. Perhaps this is why he was content to live in the little log cabin with so few of the comforts of life.

But Nancy Lincoln, the young mother, did not

complain. She, too, had grown up among the rude scenes of the backwoods. She had never known better things.

And yet she was by nature refined and gentle; and people who knew her said that she was very handsome. She was a model housekeeper, too; and her poor log cabin was the neatest and best-kept house in all that neighborhood.

No woman could be busier than she. She knew how to spin and weave, and she made all the clothing for her family.

She knew how to wield the ax and the hoe; and she could work on the farm or in the garden when her help was needed.

She had also learned how to shoot with a rifle; and she could bring down a deer or other wild game with as much ease as could her husband. And when the game was brought home, she could dress it, she could cook the flesh for food, and of the skins she could make clothing for her husband and children.

There was still another thing that she could do—she could read; and she read all the books that she could get hold of. She taught her husband the letters of the alphabet ; and she showed him how to write his name. For Thomas Lincoln had never gone to school, and he had never learned how to read.

As soon as little Abraham Lincoln was old enough to understand, his mother read stories to him from the Bible. Then, while he was still very young, she taught him to read the stories for himself.

The neighbors thought it a wonderful thing that so small a boy could read. There were very few of them who could do as much. Few of them thought it of any great use to learn how to read.

There were no school-houses in that part of Kentucky in those days, and of course there were no public schools.

One winter a traveling schoolmaster came that way. He got leave to use a cabin not far from Mr. Lincoln's, and gave notice that he would teach school for two or three weeks. The people were too poor to pay him for teaching longer.

The name of this schoolmaster was Zachariah Riney.

The young people for miles around flocked to the school. Most of them were big boys and girls, and a few were grown up young men. The only little child was Abraham Lincoln, and he was not yet five years old.

There was only one book studied at that school, and it was a spelling-book. It had some easy reading lessons at the end, but these were not to be read until after every word in the book had been spelled.

You can imagine how the big boys and girls felt when Abraham Lincoln proved that he could spell and read better than any of them.

II.—WORK AND SORROW.

In the autumn, just after Abraham Lincoln was eight years old, his parents left their Kentucky home and moved to Spencer county, in Indiana.

It was not yet a year since Indiana had become

a state.   Land could be bought very cheap, and Mr. Lincoln thought that he could make a good. living there for his family.   He had heard also that game was plentiful in the Indiana woods.

It was not more than seventy or eighty miles from the old home to the new.   But it seemed very far, indeed, and it was a good many days before the slow-moving wagon reached its journey's end. Over a part of the way there was no road, and the movers had to cut a path for themselves through the thick woods.

The boy, Abraham, was tall and very strong for his age.   He already knew how to handle an ax, and few men could shoot with a rifle better than he.   He was his father's helper in all kinds of work.

It was in November when the family came to the place which was to be their future home. Winter was near at hand.   There was no house, nor shelter of any kind.   What would become of the patient, tired mother, and the gentle little sister, who had borne themselves so bravely during the long, hard journey ?

No sooner had the horses been loosed from the wagon than Abraham and his father were at work with their axes. In a short time they had built what they called a " camp."

This camp was but a rude shed, made of poles and thatched with leaves and branches. It was enclosed on three sides, so that the chill winds or the driving rains from the north and west could not enter. The fourth side was left open, and in front of it a fire was built.

This fire was kept burning all the time. It warmed the interior of the camp. A big iron kettle was hung over it by means of a chain and pole, and in this kettle the fat bacon, the venison, the beans, and the corn were boiled for the family's dinner and supper. In the hot ashes the good mother baked luscious " corn dodgers," and sometimes, perhaps, a few potatoes.

In one end of the camp were the few cooking utensils and little articles of furniture which even the poorest house cannot do without. The rest of the space was the family sitting-room and bed-room. The floor was covered with leaves, and on these were spread the furry skins of deer and bears, and other animals.

It was in this camp that the family spent their first winter in Indiana. How very cold and dreary that winter must have been! Think of the stormy nights, of the shrieking wind, of the snow and the sleet and the bitter frost! It is not much wonder if, before the spring months came, the mother's strength began to fail.

But it was a busy winter for Thomas Lincoln. Every day his ax was heard in the woods. He was clearing the ground, so that in the spring it might be planted with corn and vegetables.

He was hewing logs for his new house; for he had made up his mind, now, to have something better than a cabin.

The woods were full of wild animals. It was easy for Abraham and his father to kill plenty of game, and thus keep the family supplied with fresh meat.

And Abraham, with chopping and hewing and hunting and trapping, was very busy for a little boy. He had but little time to play; and, since he had no playmates, we cannot know whether he even wanted to play.

With his mother, he read over and over the Bible stories which both of them loved so well. And, during the cold, stormy days, when he could not leave the camp, his mother taught him how to write.

In the spring the new house was raised. It was only a hewed log house, with one room below and a loft above. But it was so much better than the old cabin in Kentucky that it seemed like a palace.

The family had become so tired of living in the " camp," that they moved into the new house before the floor was laid, or any door hung at the doorway.

Then came the plowing and the planting and the hoeing. Everybody was busy from daylight to dark. There were so many trees and stumps that there was but little room for the corn to grow.

The summer passed, and autumn came. Then the poor mother's strength gave out. She could no longer go about her household duties. She had to depend more and more upon the help that her children could give her.

At length she became too feeble to leave her bed. She called her boy to her side. She put her arms about him and said : " Abraham, I am going away from you, and you will never see me again. I know that you will always be good and kind to your sister and father. Try to live as I have taught you, and to love your heavenly Father."

On the 5th of October she fell asleep, never to wake again.

Under a big sycamore tree, half a mile from the house, the neighbors dug the grave for the mother of Abraham Lincoln. And there they buried her in silence and great sorrow.

There was no minister there to conduct religious services. In all that new country there was no church ; and no holy man could be found to speak words of comfort and hope to the grieving ones around the grave.

But the boy, Abraham, remembered a traveling preacher, whom they had known in Kentucky. The name of this preacher was David Elkin. If he would only come!

And so, after all was over, the lad sat down and wrote a letter to David Elkin. He was only a child nine years old, but he believed that the good man would remember his poor mother, and come.

It was no easy task to write a letter. Paper and ink were not things of common use, as they are with us. A pen had to be made from the quill of a goose.

But at last the letter was finished and sent away. How it was carried I do not know ; for the mails were few and far between in those days, and postage was very high. It is more than likely that some friend, who was going into Kentucky, undertook to have it finally handed to the good preacher.

Months passed. The leaves were again on the trees. The wild flowers were blossoming in the woods. At last the preacher came.

He had ridden a hundred miles on horseback ;

he had forded rivers, and traveled through path-less woods ; he had dared the dangers of the wild forest : all in answer to the lad's beseeching letter.

He had no hope of reward, save that which is given to every man who does his duty. He did not know that there would come a time when the greatest preachers in the world would envy him his sad task.

And now the friends and neighbors gathered again under the great sycamore tree. The funeral sermon was preached. Hymns were sung. A prayer was offered. Words of comfort and sympathy were spoken.

From that time forward the mind of Abraham Lincoln was filled with a high and noble purpose. In his earliest childhood his mother had taught him to love truth and justice, to be honest and upright among men, and to reverence God. These lessons he never forgot.

Long afterward, when the world had come to know him as a very great man, he said : " All that I am, or hope to be, I owe to my angel mother."

III.—The New Mother.

The log house, which Abraham Lincoln called his home, was now more lonely and cheerless than before. The sunlight of his mother's presence had gone out of it forever.

His sister Sarah, twelve years old, was the housekeeper and cook. His father had not yet found time to lay a floor in the house, or to hang a door. There were great crevices between the logs, through which the wind and the rain drifted on every stormy day. There was not much comfort in such a house.

But the lad was never idle. In the long winter days, when there was no work to be done, he spent the time in reading or in trying to improve his writing.

There were very few books in the cabins of that backwoods settlement. But if Abraham Lincoln heard of one, he could not rest till he ·nad borrowed it and read it.

Another summer passed, and then another winter. Then, one day, Mr. Lincoln went on a visit to Kentucky, leaving his two children and their cousin, Dennis Hanks, at home to care for the house and the farm.

I do not know how long he stayed away, but it could not have been many weeks. One evening, the children were surprised to see a four-horse wagon draw up before the door.

Their father was in the wagon ; and by his side was a kind-faced woman ; and, sitting on the straw at the bottom of the wagon-bed, there were three well-dressed children—two girls and a boy.

And there were some grand things in the wagon, too. There were six split-bottomed chairs, a bureau with drawers, a wooden chest, and a feather bed. All these things were very wonderful to the lad and lassie who had never known the use of such luxuries.

"Abraham and Sarah," said Mr. Lincoln, as he leaped from the wagon, "I have brought you a new mother and a new brother and two new sisters."

The new mother greeted them very kindly,

and, no doubt, looked with gentle pity upon them. They were barefooted ; their scant clothing was little more than rags and tatters ; they did not look much like her own happy children, whom she had cared for so well.

And now it was not long until a great change was made in the Lincoln home. A floor was laid, a door was hung, a window was made, the crevices between the logs were daubed with clay.

The house was furnished in fine style, with the chairs and the bureau and the feather bed. The kind, new mother brought sunshine and hope into the place that had once been so cheerless.

With the young lad, Dennis Hanks, there were now six children in the family. But all were treated with the same kindness ; all had the same motherly care. And so, in the midst of much hard work, there were many pleasant days for them all.

IV.—School and Books.

Not very long after this, the people of the neighborhood made up their minds that they must have a school-house. And so, one day after harvest, the men met together and chopped down trees, and built a little low-roofed log cabin to serve for that purpose.

If you could see that cabin you would think it a queer kind of school-house. There was no floor. There was only one window, and in it were strips of greased paper pasted across, instead of glass. There were no desks, but only rough benches made of logs split in halves. In one end of the room was a huge fireplace; at the other end was the low doorway.

The first teacher was a man whose name was Azel Dorsey. The term of school was very short; for the settlers could not afford to pay him much. It was in mid-winter, for then there was no work for the big boys to do at home.

And the big boys, as well as the girls and the smaller boys, for miles around, came in to learn what they could from Azel Dorsey. The most of the children studied only spelling; but some of the larger ones learned reading and writing and arithmetic.

There were not very many scholars, for the houses in that new settlement were few and far apart. School began at an early hour in the morning, and did not close until the sun was down.

Just how Abraham Lincoln stood in his classes I do not know; but I must believe that he studied hard and did everything as well as he could. In the arithmetic which he used, he wrote these lines:

> "Abraham Lincoln,
> His hand and pen,
> He will be good,
> But God knows when."

In a few weeks, Azel Dorsey's school came to a close; and Abraham Lincoln was again as busy as ever about his father's farm. After that he attended school only two or three short terms. If all his school-days were put together they would not make a twelve-month.

But he kept on reading and studying at home. His step-mother said of him: "He read everything he could lay his hands on. When he came across a passage that struck him, he would write it down on boards, if he had no paper, and keep it until he had got paper.' Then he would copy it, look at it, commit it to memory, and repeat it."

Among the books that he read were the Bible, the *Pilgrim's Progress*, and the poems of Robert Burns. One day he walked a long distance to borrow a book of a farmer. This book was Weems's *Life of Washington*. He read as much as he could while walking home.

By that time it was dark, and so he sat down by the chimney and read by firelight until bedtime. Then he took the book to bed with him in the loft, and read by the light of a tallow candle.

In an hour the candle burned out. He laid the book in a crevice between two of the logs of the cabin, so that he might begin reading again as soon as it was daylight.

But in the night a storm came up. The rain was blown in, and the book was wet through and through.

In the morning, when Abraham awoke, he saw

what had happened.   He dried the leaves as well as he could, and then finished reading the book.

As soon as he had eaten his breakfast, he hurried to carry the book to its owner. He explained how the accident had happened.

" Mr. Crawford," he said, " I am willing to pay you for the book,   I have no money ; but, if you will let me, I will work for you until I have made its price."

Mr. Crawford thought that the book was worth seventy-five cents, and that Abraham's work would be worth about twenty-five cents a day.   And so the lad helped the farmer gather corn for three days, and thus became the owner of the delightful book.

He read the story of Washington many times over.   He carried the book with him to the field, and read it while he was following the plow.

From that time, Washington was the one great hero whom he admired.   Why could not he model his own life after that of Washington ? Why could not he also be a doer of great things for his country ?

V.—LIFE IN THE BACKWOODS.

Abraham Lincoln now set to work with a will to educate himself. His father thought that he did not need to learn anything more. He did not see that there was any good in book-learning. If a man could read and write and cipher, what more was needed ?

But the good step-mother thought differently ; and when another short term of school began in the little log school-house, all six of the children from the Lincoln cabin were among the scholars.

In a few weeks, however, the school had closed ; and the three boys were again hard at work, chopping and grubbing in Mr. Lincoln's clearings. They were good-natured, jolly young fellows, and they lightened their labor with many a joke and playful prank.

Many were the droll stories with which Abraham amused his two companions. Many were the puzzling questions that he asked. Sometimes in the evening, with the other five children around him, he would declaim some piece that he had learned ; or he would deliver a speech of his own on some subject of common interest.

If you could see him as he then appeared, you would hardly think that such a boy would ever become one of the most famous men of history. On his head he wore a cap made from the skin of a squirrel or a raccoon. Instead of trousers of cloth, he wore buckskin breeches, the legs of which were many inches too short. His shirt was of deerskin in the winter, and of homespun tow in the summer. Stockings he had none. His shoes were of heavy cowhide, and were worn only on Sundays or in very cold weather.

The family lived in such a way as to need very little money. Their bread was made of corn meal. Their meat was chiefly the flesh of wild game found in the forest.

Pewter plates and wooden trenchers were used on the table. The tea and coffee cups were of painted tin. There was no stove, and all the cooking was done on the hearth of the big fireplace.

But poverty was no hindrance to Abraham Lincoln. He kept on with his reading and his studies as best he could. Sometimes he would go to the little village of Gentryville, near by, to spend an evening. He would tell so many jokes and so many funny stories, that all the people would gather round him to listen.

When he was sixteen years old he went one day to Booneville, fifteen miles away, to attend a trial in court. He had never been in court before. He listened with great attention to all that was said. When the lawyer for the defense made his speech, the youth was so full of delight that he could not contain himself.

He arose from his seat, walked across the court-room, and shook hands with the lawyer. "That was the best speech I ever heard," he said.

He was tall and very slim; he was dressed in a jeans coat and buckskin trousers; his feet were bare. It must have been a strange sight to see him thus complimenting an old and practiced lawyer.

From that time, one ambition seemed to fill his mind. He wanted to be a lawyer and make great speeches in court. He walked twelve miles barefooted, to borrow a copy of the laws of Indiana. Day and night he read and studied.

"Some day I shall be President of the United States," he said to some of his young friends. And this he said not as a joke, but in the firm belief that it would prove to be true.

VI.—The Boatman.

One of Thomas Lincoln's friends owned a ferry-boat on the Ohio River. It was nothing but a small rowboat, and would carry only three or four people at a time. This man wanted to employ some one to take care of his boat and to ferry people across the river.

Thomas Lincoln was in need of money; and so he arranged with his friend for Abraham to do this work. The wages of the young man were to be $2.50 a week. But all the money was to be his father's.

One day two strangers came to the landing. They wanted to take passage on a steamboat that was coming down the river. The ferry-boy signalled to the steamboat and it stopped in mid-stream. Then the boy rowed out with the two passengers, and they were taken on board.

Just as he was turning towards the shore again, each of the strangers tossed a half-dollar into his boat. He picked the silver up and looked at it. Ah, how rich he felt! He had never had so much money at one time. And he had gotten all for a few minutes' labor!

When winter came on, there were fewer people who wanted to cross the river. So, at last, the ferry-boat was tied up, and Abraham Lincoln went back to his father's home.

He was now nineteen years old. He was very tall—nearly six feet four inches in height. He was as strong as a young giant. He could jump higher and farther, and he could run faster, than any of his fellows; and there was no one, far or near, who could lay him on his back.

Although he had always lived in a community of rude, rough people, he had no bad habits. He used no tobacco; he did not drink strong liquor; no profane word ever passed his lips.

He was good-natured at all times, and kind to every one.

During that winter, Mr. Gentry, the store-keeper in the village, had bought a good deal of corn and pork. He intended, in the spring, to load this on a flatboat and send it down the river to New Orleans.

In looking about for a captain to take charge of the boat, he happened to think of Abraham Lincoln. He knew that he could trust the young man. And so a bargain was soon made. Abraham agreed to pilot the boat to New Orleans and to market the produce there; and Mr. Gentry was to pay his father eight dollars and a half a month for his services.

As soon as the ice had well melted from the river, the voyage was begun. Besides Captain Lincoln there was only one man in the crew, and that was a son of Mr. Gentry's.

The voyage was a long and weary one, but at last the two boatmen reached the great southern city. Here they saw many strange things of which they had never heard before. But they soon sold their cargo and boat, and then returned home on a steamboat.

To Abraham Lincoln the world was now very different from what it had seemed before. He longed to be away from the narrow life in the woods of Spencer county. He longed to be doing something for himself—to be making for himself a fortune and a name.

But then he remembered his mother's teachings when he sat on her knee in the old Kentucky home, "Always do right." He remembered her last words, "I know you will be kind to your father."

And so he resolved to stay with his father, to work for him, and to give him all his earnings until he was twenty-one years old.

VII.—THE FIRST YEARS IN ILLINOIS.

Early in the spring of 1830, Thomas Lincoln sold his farm in Indiana, and the whole family moved to Illinois. The household goods were put in a wagon drawn by four yoke of oxen.

The kind step-mother and her daughters rode also in the wagon.

Abraham Lincoln, with a long whip in his hand, trudged through the mud by the side of the road and guided the oxen. Who that saw him thus going into Illinois would have dreamed that he would in time become that state's greatest citizen?

The journey was a long and hard one; but in two weeks they reached Decatur, where they had decided to make their new home.

Abraham Lincoln was now over twenty-one years old. He was his own man. But he stayed with his father that spring. He helped him fence his land; he helped him plant his corn.

But his father had no money to give him. The young man's clothing was all worn out, and he had nothing with which to buy any more. What should he do?

Three miles from his father's cabin there lived a thrifty woman, whose name was Nancy Miller. Mrs. Miller owned a flock of sheep, and in her house there were a spinning-wheel and a loom that were always busy. And so you must know that she wove a great deal of jeans and home-made cloth.

Abraham Lincoln bargained with this woman to make him a pair of trousers. He agreed that for each yard of cloth required, he would split for her four hundred rails.

He had to split fourteen hundred rails in all; but he worked so fast that he had finished them before the trousers were ready.

The next April saw young Lincoln piloting another flatboat down the Mississippi to New Orleans. His companion this time was his mother's relative, John Hanks. This time he stayed longer in New Orleans, and he saw some things which he had barely noticed on his first trip.

He saw gangs of slaves being driven through the streets. He visited the slave-market, and saw women and girls sold to the highest bidder like so many cattle.

The young man, who would not be unkind to any living being, was shocked by these sights. " His heart bled ; he was mad, thoughtful, sad, and depressed."

He said to John Hanks, "If I ever get a chance to hit that institution, I'll hit it hard, John."

He came back from New Orleans in July. Mr. Offut, the owner of the flatboat which he had taken down, then employed him to act as clerk in a country store which he had at New Salem.

New Salem was a little town not far from Springfield.

Young Lincoln was a good salesman, and all the customers liked him. Mr. Offut declared that the young man knew more than anyone else in the United States, and that he could outrun and outwrestle any man in the county.

But in the spring of the next year Mr. Offut failed. The store was closed, and Abraham Lincoln was out of employment again.

VIII.—THE BLACK HAWK WAR.

There were still a good many Indians in the West. The Sac Indians had lately sold their lands in northern Illinois to the United States. They had then moved across the Mississippi river, to other lands that had been set apart for them.

But they did not like their new home. At last they made up their minds to go back to their former hunting-grounds. They were led by a chief whose name was Black Hawk; and they began by killing the white settlers and burning their houses and crops.

This was in the spring of 1832.

The whole state of Illinois was in alarm. The governor called for volunteers to help the United States soldiers drive the Indians back.

Abraham Lincoln enlisted. His company elected him captain.

He did not know anything about military tactics. He did not know how to give orders to his men. But he did the best that he could, and learned a great deal by experience.

His company marched northward and westward until they came to the Mississippi river. But they did not meet any Indians, and so there was no fighting.

The young men under Captain Lincoln were

rude fellows from the prairies and backwoods. They were rough in their manners, and hard to control. But they had very high respect for their captain.

Perhaps this was because of his great strength, and his skill in wrestling ; for he could put the roughest and strongest of them on their backs. Perhaps it was because he was good-natured and kind, and, at the same time, very firm and decisive.

In a few weeks the time for which the company had enlisted came to an end. The young men were tired of being soldiers ; and so all, except Captain Lincoln and one man, were glad to hurry home.

But Captain Lincoln never gave up anything half done. He enlisted again. This time he was a private in a company of mounted rangers.

The main camp of the volunteers and soldiers was on the banks of the Rock river, in northern Illinois.

Here, one day, Abraham Lincoln saw a young lieutenant of the United States army, whose name was Jefferson Davis. It is not likely that the fine young officer noticed the rough-clad ranger ; but they were to know more of each other at a future time.

Three weeks after that the war was at an end. The Indians had been beaten in a battle, and Black Hawk had been taken prisoner.

But Abraham Lincoln had not been in any fight. He had not seen any Indians, except peaceable ones.

In June his company was mustered out, and he returned home to New Salem.

He was then twenty-three years old.

IX.—In the Legislature.

When Abraham Lincoln came back to New Salem it was nearly time for the state election. The people of the town and neighborhood wanted to send him to the legislature, and he agreed to be a candidate.

It was at Pappsville, twelve miles from Springfield, that he made his first campaign speech.

He said : " Gentlemen and fellow-citizens—

" I presume you all know who I am.

" I am humble Abraham Lincoln. I have been solicited by my friends to become a candidate for the legislature.

" My politics are short and sweet.

" I am in favor of a national bank ; am in favor of the internal improvement system, and a high protective tariff.

" These are my sentiments and political principles. If elected, I shall be thankful ; if not, it will be all the same."

He was a tall, gawky, rough-looking fellow. He was dressed in a coarse suit of homespun, much the worse for wear.

A few days after that, he made a longer and better speech at Springfield.

But he was not elected.

About this time a worthless fellow, whose name was Berry, persuaded Mr. Lincoln to help him buy a store in New Salem. Mr. Lincoln had no money, but he gave his notes for the value of half the goods,

The venture was not a profitable one. In a few months the store was sold ; but Abraham did not receive a dollar for it. It was six years before he was able to pay off the notes which he had given.

During all this time Mr. Lincoln did not give up the idea of being a lawyer. He bought a second-hand copy of *Blackstone's Commentaries* at auction. He studied it so diligently that in a few weeks he had mastered the whole of it.

He bought an old form-book, and began to draw up contracts, deeds, and all kinds of legal papers.

He would often walk to Springfield, fourteen miles away, to borrow a book ; and he would master thirty or forty pages of it while returning home.

Soon he began to practice in a small way before justices of the peace and country juries. He was appointed postmaster at New Salem, but so little mail came to the place that the office was soon discontinued.

He was nearly twenty-five years old. But,

with all his industry, he could hardly earn money enough to pay for his board and clothing.

He had learned a little about surveying while living in Indiana. He now took up the study again, and was soon appointed deputy surveyor of Sangamon county.

He was very skilful as a surveyor. Although his chain was only a grape-vine, he was very accurate and never made mistakes.

The next year he was again a candidate for the legislature. This time the people were ready to vote for him, and he was elected. It was no small thing for so young a man to be chosen to help make the laws of his state.

No man ever had fewer advantages than Abraham Lincoln. As a boy, he was the poorest of the poor. No rich friend held out a helping hand. But see what he had already accomplished by pluck, perseverance, and honesty!

He had not had access to many books, but he knew books better than most men of his age. He knew the Bible by heart; he was familiar with Shakespeare; he could repeat nearly all the poems of Burns; he knew much about physics and mechanics; he had mastered the elements of law.

He was very awkward and far from handsome, but he was so modest, so unselfish and kind, that every one who knew him liked him. He was a true gentleman—a gentleman at heart, if not in outside polish.

And so, as I have already said, Abraham Lincoln, at the age of twenty-five, was elected to the state legislature. He served the people so well that when his term closed, two years later, they sent him back for another term.

The capital of Illinois had, up to this time, been at Vandalia. Mr. Lincoln and his friends now succeeded in having a law passed to remove it to Springfield. Springfield was nearer to the centre of the state; it was more convenient to everybody, and had other advantages which Vandalia did not have.

The people of Springfield were so delighted that they urged Mr. Lincoln to come there and practice law. An older lawyer, whose name was

John T. Stuart, and who had a good practice, offered to take him in partnership with him.

And so, in 1837, Abraham Lincoln left New Salem and removed to Springfield.   He did not have much to move.   All the goods that he had in the world were a few clothes, which he carried in a pair of saddle-bags, and two or three law books.   He had no money, and he rode into Springfield on a borrowed horse.

He was then twenty-eight years old.

From that time on, Springfield was his home.

X.—Politics and Marriage.

The next year after his removal to Springfield, Mr. Lincoln was elected to the legislature for the third time.

There were then, in this country, two great political parties, the Democrats and the Whigs. Mr. Lincoln was a Whig, and he soon became the leader of his party in the state.   But the Whigs were not so strong as the Democrats.

The legislature was in session only a few weeks

each year ; and so Mr. Lincoln could devote all the rest of the time to the practice of law. There were many able lawyers in Illinois ; but Abe Lincoln of Springfield soon made himself known among the best of them.

In 1840, he was again elected to the legislature. This was the year in which General William H. Harrison was elected president of the United States. General Harrison was a Whig ; and Mr. Lincoln's name was on the Whig ticket as a candidate for presidential elector in his state.

The presidential campaign was one of the most exciting that had ever been known. It was called the " log cabin " campaign, because General Harrison had lived in a log cabin, and his opponents had sneered at his poverty.

In the East as well as in the West, the excitement was very great. In every city and town and village, wherever there was a political meeting, a log cabin was seen. On one side of the low door hung a long-handled gourd ; on the other side, a coon-skin was nailed to the logs ;

the blue smoke curled up from the top of the stick-and-clay chimney.

You may believe that Abraham Lincoln went into this campaign with all his heart. He traveled over a part of the state, making stump-speeches for his party.

One of his ablest opponents was a young lawyer, not quite his own age, whose name was Stephen A. Douglas. In many places, during this campaign, Lincoln and Douglas met in public debate upon the questions of the day. And both of them were so shrewd; so well informed, and so eloquent, that those who heard them were unable to decide which was the greater of the two.

General Harrison was elected, but not through the help of Mr. Lincoln; for the vote of Illinois that year was for the Democratic candidate.

In 1842, when he was thirty-three years old, Mr. Lincoln was married to Miss Mary Todd, a young lady from Kentucky, who had lately come to Springfield on a visit.

For some time after their marriage, Mr. and

The Birthplace
Monument at Springfield.
Residence at Springfield Ill.

Mrs. Lincoln lived in a hotel called the " Globe Tavern," paying four dollars a week for rooms and board. But, in 1844, Mr. Lincoln bought a small, but comfortable frame house, and in this they lived until they went to the White House, seventeen years later.

Although he had been successful as a young lawyer, Mr. Lincoln was still a poor man. But Mrs. Lincoln said : "I would rather have a good man, a man of mind, with bright prospects for success and power and fame, than marry one with all the horses and houses and gold in the world."

XI.—Congressman and Lawyer.

In 1846, Mr. Lincoln was again elected to the legislature.

In the following year the people of his district chose him to be their representative in Congress. He took his seat in December. He was then thirty-nine years old. He was the only Whig from Illinois.

There were many famous men in Congress at

that time. Mr. Lincoln's life-long rival, Stephen A. Douglas, was one of the senators from Illinois. He had already served a term or two in the House of Representatives.

Daniel Webster was also in the Senate ; and so was John C. Calhoun ; and so was Jefferson Davis.

Mr. Lincoln took an active interest in all the subjects that came before Congress. He made many speeches. But, perhaps, the most important thing that he did at this time was to propose a bill for the abolition of the slave-trade in the city of Washington.

He believed that slavery was unjust to the slave and harmful to the nation. He wanted to do what he could to keep it from becoming a still greater evil. But the bill was opposed so strongly that it was not even voted upon.

After the close of Mr. Lincoln's term in Congress, he hoped that President Taylor, who was a Whig, might appoint him to a good office. But in this he was disappointed.

And so, in 1849, he returned to his home in

Springfield, and again settled down to the practice of law.

He was then forty years old. Considering the poverty of his youth, he had done great things for himself. But he had not done much for his country. Outside of his own state his name was still unknown.

His life for the next few years was like that of any other successful lawyer in the newly-settled West. He had a large practice, but his fees were very small. His income from his profession was seldom more than $2,000 a year.

His habits were very simple. He lived comfortably and respectably. In his modest little home there was an air of order and refinement, but no show of luxury.

No matter where he might go, Mr. Lincoln would have been known as a Western man. He was six feet four inches in height. His face was very homely, but very kind.

He was cordial and friendly in his manners. There was something about him which made everybody feel that he was a sincere, truthful,

upright man.   He was known among his neighbors as "Honest Abe Lincoln."

XII.—THE QUESTION OF SLAVERY.

The great subject before the country at this time was slavery.   It had been the cause of trouble for many years.

In the early settlement of the American colonies, slavery had been introduced through the influence of the English government.   The first slaves had been brought to Virginia nearly 240 years before the time of which I am telling you.

Many people saw from the beginning that it was an evil which would at some distant day bring disaster upon the country.   In 1772, the people of Virginia petitioned the king of England to put a stop to the bringing of slaves from Africa into that colony.   But the petition was rejected ; and the king forbade them to speak of the matter any more.

Washington, Jefferson, and other founders of our nation looked upon slavery as an evil.   They hoped that the time might come when it would be done away with; for they knew that the country would prosper better without it.

At the time of the Revolution, slavery was permitted in all the states. But it was gradually abolished, first in Pennsylvania and then in the New England states, and afterwards in New York.

In 1787, a law was passed by Congress declaring that there should be no slavery in the territory northwest of the river Ohio. This was the territory from which the states of Ohio, Indiana, Illinois, Michigan, and Wisconsin were formed; and so, of course, these states were free states from the beginning.

The great industry of the South was cotton-raising. The people of the Southern states claimed that slavery was necessary, because only negro slaves could do the work required on the big cotton plantations. Kentucky, Tennessee, Alabama, Mississippi, and Louisiana were admitted, one by one, into the Union; and all were slave states.

In 1821, Missouri applied for admission into the

Union. The South wanted slavery in this state also, but the North objected. There were many hot debates in Congress over this question. At last, through the influence of Henry Clay, the dispute was settled by what has since been known as the Missouri Compromise.

The Missouri Compromise provided that Missouri should be a slave state ; this was to satisfy the South. On the other hand, it declared that all the western territory north of the line which formed the southern boundary of Missouri, should forever be free ; this was to appease the North.

But the cotton planters of the South grew more wealthy by the labor of their slaves. More territory was needed for the extension of slavery. Texas joined the United States and became a slave state.

Then followed a war with Mexico ; and California, New Mexico and Utah were taken from that country. Should slavery be allowed in these new territories also ?

At this time a new political party was formed.

It was called the "Free Soil Party," and the principle for which it contended was this : "*No more slave states and no slave territory.*"

This party was not very strong at first, but soon large numbers of Whigs and many northern Democrats, who did not believe in the extension of slavery, began to join it.

Although the Whig party refused to take any position against the extension of slavery, there were many anti-slavery Whigs who still remained with it and voted the Whig ticket—and one of these men was Abraham Lincoln.

The contest between freedom and slavery became more fierce every day. At last another compromise was proposed by Henry Clay.

This compromise provided that California should be admitted as a free state ; that slavery should not be prohibited in New Mexico and Utah ; that there should be no more markets for slaves in the District of Columbia ; and that a new and very strict fugitive-slave law should be passed.

This compromise is called the "Compromise

of 1850." It was in support of these measures
that Daniel Webster made his last great speech.

It was hoped by Webster and Clay that the
Compromise of 1850 would put an end to the
agitation about slavery. "Now we shall have
peace," they said. But the agitation became
stronger and stronger, and peace seemed farther
away than ever before.

In 1854, a bill was passed by Congress to or-
ganize the territories of Kansas and Nebraska.
This bill provided that the Missouri Compromise
should be repealed, and that the question of
slavery in these territories should be decided by
the people living in them.

The bill was passed through the influence of
Stephen A. Douglas of Illinois. There was now
no bar to the extension of slavery into any of
the territories save that of public opinion.

The excitement all over the North was very
great. In Kansas there was actual war between
those who favored slavery and those who opposed it. Thinking men in all parts of the country saw that a great crisis was at hand.

XIII.—LINCOLN AND DOUGLAS.

It was then that Abraham Lincoln came forward as the champion of freedom.

Stephen A. Douglas was a candidate for re-election to the Senate, and he found it necessary to defend himself before the people of his state for the part he had taken in repealing the Missouri Compromise. He went from one city to another, making speeches; and at each place Abraham Lincoln met him in joint debate.

"I do not care whether slavery is voted into or out of the territories," said Mr. Douglas. "The question of slavery is one of climate. Wherever it is to the interest of the inhabitants of a territory to have slave property, there a slave law will be enacted."

But Mr. Lincoln replied, "The men who signed the Declaration of Independence said that all men are created equal, and are endowed by their Creator with certain inalienable rights— life, liberty, and the pursuit of happiness. . . . I beseech you, do not destroy that immortal emblem of humanity, the Declaration of Independence."

At last, Mr. Douglas felt that he was beaten. He proposed that both should go home, and that there should be no more joint discussions. Mr. Lincoln agreed to this; but the words which he had spoken sank deep into the hearts of those who heard them.

The speeches of Lincoln and Douglas were printed in a book. People in all parts of the country read them. They had heard much about Stephen A. Douglas. He was called "The Little Giant." He had long been famous among the politicians of the country. It was believed that he would be the next President of the United States.

But who was this man Lincoln, who had so bravely vanquished the Little Giant? He was called "Honest Abe." There were few people outside of his state who had ever heard of him before.

Mr. Douglas returned to his seat in the United States Senate. Mr. Lincoln became the acknowledged leader of the forces opposed to the extension of slavery.

In May, 1856, a convention of the people of Illinois was held in Bloomington, Illinois. It met for the purpose of forming a new political party, the chief object and aim of which should be to oppose the extension of slavery into the territories.

Mr. Lincoln made a speech to the members of this convention. It was one of the greatest speeches ever heard in this country. "Again and again, during the delivery, the audience sprang to their feet, and, by long-continued cheers, expressed how deeply the speaker had roused them."

And so the new party was organized. It was composed of the men who had formed the old Free Soil Party, together with such Whigs and Democrats as were opposed to the further growth of the slave power. But the greater number of its members were Whigs. This new party was called The Republican Party.

In June, the Republican Party held a national

convention at Philadelphia, and nominated John C. Frémont for President. But the party was not strong enough to carry the election that year.

In that same month the Democrats held a convention at Cincinnati. Every effort was made to nominate Stephen A. Douglas for President. But he was beaten in his own party, on account of the action which he had taken in the repeal of the Missouri Compromise.

James Buchanan was nominated in his stead, and, in November, was elected.

And so the conflict went on.

In the year 1858 there was another series of joint debates between Lincoln and Douglas. Both were candidates for the United States Senate. Their speeches were among the most remarkable ever delivered in any country.

Lincoln spoke for liberty and justice. Douglas's speeches were full of fire and patriotism. He hoped to be elected President in 1860. In the end, it was generally acknowledged that Lincoln had made the best arguments. But Douglas was re-elected to the Senate.

XIV.—President of the United States.

In 1860 there were four candidates for the presidency.

The great Democratic Party was divided into two branches. One branch nominated Stephen A. Douglas. The other branch, which included the larger number of the slave-owners of the South, nominated John C. Breckinridge, of Kentucky.

The remnant of the old Whig Party, now called the " Union Party," nominated John Bell, of Tennessee.

The Republican Party nominated Abraham Lincoln.

In November came the election, and a majority of all the electors chosen were for Lincoln.

The people of the cotton-growing states believed that, by this election, the Northern people intended to deprive them of their rights. They believed that the anti-slavery people intended to do much more than prevent the extension of slavery. They believed that the abolitionists were bent upon passing laws to deprive them of their slaves.

Wild rumors were circulated concerning the designs which the " Black Republicans," as they were called, had formed for their coercion and oppression. They declared that they would never submit.

And so, in December, the people of South Carolina met in convention, and declared that that state had seceded from the Union—that they would no longer be citizens of the United States. One by one, six other states followed ; and they united to form a new government, called the Confederate States of America.

It had long been held by the men of the South that a state had the right to withdraw from the Union at any time. This was called the doctrine of States' Rights.

The Confederate States at once chose Jefferson Davis for their President, and declared themselves free and independent.

In February, Mr. Lincoln went to Washington to be inaugurated. His enemies openly boasted that he should never reach that city alive; and a plot was formed to kill him on his passage through Baltimore. But he took an earlier train than the one appointed, and arrived at the capital in safety.

On the 4th of March he was inaugurated. In his address at that time he said: "In your hands, my dissatisfied countrymen, and not in mine, is the momentous issue of civil war. Your government will not assail you. You can have no conflict without being yourselves the aggressors. You have no oath registered in heaven to destroy the government; while I shall have the most solemn one to protect and defend it."

The Confederate States demanded that the government should give up all the forts, arsenals, and public property within their limits. This, President Lincoln refused to do. He said that he could not admit that these states had withdrawn from the Union, or that they could withdraw without the consent of the people of the United States, given in a national convention.

And so, in April, the Confederate guns were

turned upon Fort Sumter in Charleston harbor, and the war was begun. President Lincoln issued a call for 75,000 men to serve in the army for three months ; and both parties prepared for the great contest.

It is not my purpose to give a history of that terrible war of four years. The question of slavery was now a secondary one. The men of one party were determined, at whatever hazard, to preserve the Union. The men of the other party fought to defend their doctrine of States' Rights, and to set up an independent government of their own.

President Lincoln was urged to use his power and declare all the slaves free. He answered :

" My paramount object is to save the Union, and not either to save or destroy slavery.

" If I could save the Union without freeing any slave, I would do it. If I could save it by freeing all the slaves, I would do it. If I could save it by freeing some and leaving others alone, I would also do that."

At last, however, when he saw that the success of the Union arms depended upon his freeing the slaves, he decided to do so. On the 1st of January, 1863, he issued a proclamation declaring that the slaves, in all the states or parts of states then in rebellion, should be free.

By this proclamation, more than three millions of colored people were given their freedom.

But the war still went on. It reached a turning point, however, at the battle of Gettysburg, in July, that same year. From that time the cause of the Confederate States was on the wane. Little by little the patriots, who were struggling for the preservation of the Union, prevailed.

XIV.—The End of a Great Life.

At the close of Mr. Lincoln's first term, he was again elected President of the United States. The war was still going on, but the Union arms were now everywhere victorious.

His second inaugural address was very short. He did not boast of any of his achievements; he did not rejoice over the defeat of his enemies. But he said:

" With malice toward none ; with charity for all ; with firmness in the right, as God gives us to see the right, let us strive on to finish the work we are in ; to bind up the nation's wounds ; to care for him who shall have borne the battle, and for his widow and his orphan—to do all which may achieve and cherish a just and lasting peace among ourselves and with all nations."

Five weeks after that, on the 9th of April, 1865, the Confederate army surrendered, and the war was at an end.

Abraham Lincoln's work was done.

The 14th of April was Good Friday. On the evening of that day, Mr. Lincoln, with Mrs. Lincoln and two or three friends, visited Ford's Theatre in Washington.

At a few minutes past 10 o'clock, an actor whose name was John Wilkes Booth, came into the box where Mr. Lincoln sat. No one saw him enter. He pointed a pistol at the President's head, and fired. He leaped down upon the stage, shouting " *Sic semper tyrannus !* The

South is avenged!" Then he ran behind the scenes and out by the stage door.

The President fell forward. His eyes closed. He neither saw, nor heard, nor felt anything that was taking place. Kind arms carried him to a private house not far away.

At twenty minutes past seven o'clock the next morning, those who watched beside him gave out the mournful news that Abraham Lincoln was dead.

He was fifty-six years old.

The whole nation wept for him. In the South as well as in the North, the people bowed themselves in grief. Heartfelt tributes of sorrow came from other lands in all parts of the world. Never, before nor since, has there been such universal mourning.

Such is the story of Abraham Lincoln. In the history of the world, there is no story more full of lessons of perseverance, of patience, of honor, of true nobility of purpose. Among the great men of all time, there has been no one more truly great than he.